OUR COUNTRY FOR THE SAKE OF THE WORLD.

A

SERMON

IN BEHALF OF THE

AMERICAN HOME MISSIONARY SOCIETY,

PREACHED IN THE CITIES OF NEW YORK AND BROOKLYN,

MAY, 1851,

BY

REV. DAVID H. RIDDLE, D.D.,

PITTSBURGH, PA.

NEW YORK:

PRINTED FOR THE AMERICAN HOME MISSIONARY SOCIETY,

BY BAKER, GODWIN & CO.,

No. 1 Spruce Street.

1851.

SERMON.

PSALM 67: 1, 2.

GOD BE MERCIFUL UNTO US, AND BLESS US, AND CAUSE HIS FACE TO SHINE UPON US.

THAT THY WAY MAY BE KNOWN UPON EARTH, THY SAVING HEALTH AMONG ALL NATIONS.

The beautiful principle embodied in these words, we propose, on this occasion, to apply to the subject of Home Missions; for rightly understood, we think it places that enterprise in its most attractive and sublime relations. This principle, if we have apprehended it, is, that the establishment and prevalence of right religious influences and institutions in our own land, is the surest and speediest method of securing the evangelization of the world. The principle originally applied, of course, to those who lived under the Old Testament dispensation. This Psalm belonged to the liturgical service of the Jewish church; and was a portion, therefore, not merely of the private devotional reading of that people, but of their public religious education. It was designed and adapted to develop a proper spirit in the mass of the people, and to shape the genius of the ancient church.

The peculiar structure of the passage shows the close relation existing between the spiritual prosperity of God's ancient people, and the salvation of the nations of the earth. "God be merciful unto us, and bless us, and cause his face to shine upon us." In these words is acknowledged God's blessing as the true source of national excellence and prosperity, and the only security of their glorious institutions. But why did they so earnestly desire this blessing and the perpetuity of their national institutions? "That thy way"—God's revealed method of salvation—"may be known on earth, thy saving health"—God's means of curing the moral maladies of man—"among all nations." "God shall bless us, and all the ends of the earth shall fear him." This view of the passage, which accords, we think, with all just principles of philosophy, exhibits the ancient church in a lovely, to some, possibly in a novel aspect. Even in the ancient church, when under tutors and governors, till the times appointed by the Father, there was cultivated an expansive benevolence, which embraced the wants and wretchedness of the race—a spirit which taught them to esteem themselves trustees of the blessings of God's salvation for "all nations." To every child of Abraham his native land was peculiarly lovely, associated as it was in every hill and valley with so many glorious recollections of the past; the land of promise, where the battles of the Lord had been fought by the heroes of faith; where the bones of the Patriarchs reposed; where the Ark of the Covenant dwelt, and the Shekinah appeared. In their jubilees piety and patriotism blended in the rapturous cry, "He hath not dealt so with any nation." But when the true spirit of the dispensation of types and shadows was imbibed, their country, the glory of all lands, was most glorious in its destined relations to God's plans towards the world,—loveliest, as the chosen centre whence the "lines" of "saving health" should "go forth through all the earth," and bless and beautify "all nations." A genuine patriotism baptized with the spirit of religion, became, as it always must, a blessed and world-wide philanthropy. In his nation and country was embosomed, and afterwards manifested, "a light" which was to lighten the Gentiles, as well as be "the glory of his people Israel." When the church should obey the voice of her Lord, "Arise, shine, for thy light is come, and the glory of the Lord is risen upon thee," then nations would come to her light, and kings to the brightness of her rising. The forces of the Gentiles, the abundance of the sea, the flocks of Kedar, the rams of Nebaioth, gold and incense, the fir-tree, the pine-tree, and the box together,—the peculiar products of every clime and the glory of every kindred, were to beautify his sanctuary, and make the place of his feet glorious. And for this purpose, to them were intrusted the Oracles of God, and to them pertained the adoption, and the glory, and the covenants, and the giving of the Law, and the service of God, and the promises. Theirs were the fathers, of whom, as concerning the flesh, Christ came, who is over all, God blessed forever.

A Jew, rightly trained by the inner spirit and genius of this dispensation, would therefore prize his institutions, and pray for their continuance; would most earnestly of all desire God's blessing, the sunshine of his face and favor on his native land, for the sake and salvation of others, yea of "*all nations.*" "God be merciful unto us, and bless us, and cause his face to shine upon us, that thy way may be known upon earth, thy saving health among all nations." "As the new wine is found in the cluster," potentially and in purpose, and one saith, "destroy it not, for a blessing is in it," the Jew would rejoice that one whose word was omnipotent for preservation, had said this of his land and nation, because in it, to God's eye and the eye of faith, was found an element, not yet indeed matured, the new wine of the kingdom of God, which yet all nations were to drink for refreshment and salvation—the prelibation of a nobler cup at the marriage supper of the Lamb.

Brethren, as Americans, and especially as American Christians, we are privileged as was the ancient Jew, and for analogous reasons, to love our country, and to pray for God's blessing and the sunshine of his favor on our native land! Patriotism, without boastful presumption, may say, "He hath not dealt so with any nation." God never made such another country as ours. The sun, as he goes careering and rejoicing as a strong man to run his race, from the one end of heaven to the other, does not shine on another land like this. Yes! we may, and for good and substantial reasons, LOVE OUR COUNTRY. But there is a nobler sentiment which should be enkindled in every soul, and incorporated with every passion, and refine and ennoble every thought and feeling and action of all our mighty population—OUR COUNTRY FOR THE SAKE AND SALVATION OF OUR WORLD. If we are true to our mission, and imbibe the spirit of our Master, and walk worthy of the manhood of the church, and be not rebuked by the manifestations even of its pupilage; American patriotism, baptized by piety, must become a blessed world-embracing—world-benefiting—world-saving philanthropy!

We should seek the blessing of God on our country, and labor for its spiritual prosperity, and the universal establishment, in all our borders, of christian institutions and their collateral and consequent influences. And he is not a Christian, in deed and in truth, who does not do this to the full extent of his ability and opportunity, by his wealth, example and influence. But Oh! what an increment of motive and energy will be added to all, if we do this, as the willing instruments and conscious trustees of the great God, for the speedy and universal evangelization of our race.

On this high ground, we desire to place the enterprise, and obligations, and glory of Home Missions. We plead and labor for the establishment and extension of a sound ministry, and the evangelical influences which invariably cluster around it, beneficent to man and conservative of his interests in all his relations. By the enlargement of Home Missions, correspondently with our unparalleled enlargement of territory, and increase of population, we desire to secure the prevalence of true piety and christian principles at home; but in so doing, we are pleading and laboring for a world's redemption, for the good of a race for which Christ died, and over which he is set to reign; and thus, indirectly, indeed, but effectually and practically, we are fulfilling the injunction of the Master, "Go ye into all the world, and preach the Gospel to every creature." We try to fulfil this intensive dispensation of christianity in our land as represented by David, that so "the mustard seed," the symbol of its extension, may grow to its destined proportions, and happy spirits from all nations may sing amidst its branches, thence to take their flight, in joyous myriads, and nestle amidst the branches of the tree of life in the midst of the paradise of God, where all at last, of every tribe, and kingdom, and clime, will sing together the new song of Moses and the Lamb.

Let our whole land be leavened, our country thoroughly evangelized—let all our institutions be brought under the sanctifying influences of christian principles; let all our population, high and low, rich and poor, learned and rude, from the President who occupies the people's house, to the peasant who inhabits the lowliest hamlet or hovel of our Western wilds, be baptized with the spirit of Jesus Christ; let Christianity of a pure apostolic type, reign without a rival in all our councils, modify all our legislation, be the inspiring genius of all our commercial, agricultural, and manufacturing interests; let its precepts direct the application of our increasing and superfluous wealth, and the grace of its author guide us in projecting and prosecuting our schemes of philanthropy; let America, in a word, as the result of God's blessing on her institutions of religion and organs of benevolent action, once fully realize her responsibility to God, and see aright her mission to mankind, and the way of God would soon be known on earth, and his *saving health* would soon be experienced among all nations. Right institutions, civil and religious—the common heritage of man, and which appertain equally and inalienably to all nations, and which we hold in trust for the rest of the race, would soon be enjoyed by this dark and troubled world, tossed so long by tempests on the surges of unavailing change. The prayer of the great American church of all denominations, caught from the ancient oracle, should be, "God be merciful unto us, and bless us, and cause his face to shine upon us, that thy way may be known upon earth, thy saving health among all nations." And every one who has a heart to love God, his country and his kind, should say, Amen! For it is the prayer and response of enlightened patriotism, enlarged philanthropy, and true Christianity.

This position of Home Missions is based on the assumption of the immense influence of our country, for good or evil, on the other nations of the earth,—a postulate which we presume will be questioned by no intelligent Christian or citizen who has allowed his mind at all, or intelligently at least, to dwell upon the subject. The providence and past dealings of God seem to say to our country, "Who knoweth whether thou art come to the kingdom for such a time as this?" In the arrangements of that Being who "setteth up one and putteth down another," whether it be spoken of a nation or a man only, we have come to a position of peculiar, at least, if we cannot say peerless eminence, amongst existing nations; to the possession of extensive, if not incomparable influence, giving us incalculable power over the rest of the world. With a gladness of gratitude, not unmingled with solicitude for the fearful responsibilities involved, we gather evidences of this, alike from the acknowledgment of friends, and the unwilling but not less unequivocal admissions of our enemies; from the hopes of the struggling masses, and the fears of the dominant and oppressive minorities of the earth. And was there ever "such a time as this," when so many elements derived from the intimations of prophecy and occurrent events, combined to constitute and justify the expectations of a crisis, and when the possession of power involved such mighty responsibilities? Granting that there is to be an end, as unquestionably there is an expectation, that God—who has allowed these anticipations to be gradually formed in the great heart of humanity, deepening and becoming more definite from age to age—means to meet and fulfil them; that the scoff of an atheistic age, "all things are to continue as they were from the beginning of the creation," in never-ending cycles of expectation and disappointment, is unphilosophical, as well as untrue; do not the signs and the tendencies of the times, the voice of prophecy, the wants of the world, the deep cry of our baffled race "made subject to vanity," all seem to indicate, that soon God's "way is to be known on earth, and his saving health among all nations?" and that our country, for this purpose has been raised up, and trained, and disciplined, and preserved through all our past vicissitudes and perils as a nation?

Surely God has a purpose in so ordering events, that elements of power, at particular periods, should come into the possession of particular nations, so that they may exert a decisive influence on the destinies of the age and the fate of the world. "If thou hadst known, even thou, at least in this thy day, the things which belong unto thy peace," said the Saviour, to a nation of old; "but now they are hid from thine eyes." Thus it has been often in the past history of the world. If nations could have seen their dispensation, as we now see it—could our light have been thrown back on their path, or the issues thundered in trumpet tones, how different would have been their consciousness of their mission, and possibly, the course of their conduct.

At one period, had one more onward step been taken, Carthage, the representative of African, instead of Rome, the representative of European civilization, might have triumphed, and been mistress of the world: and at another, had some other general, instead of Grouchy, been selected, who would have scorned to taint his itching palm with gold, the tide of battle might have been turned at Waterloo, and with it, the fate of the world. God, who "hath determined the times, and the bounds of our habitations before appointed," seems to have purposed that our country, if conscious of her mission and prepared to meet it, may exert a mighty, possibly a decisive influence on the destinies of the earth, and have a glorious part assigned her amidst the last acts of the long drama of time. And shall it be said of us, "Oh! if thou hadst known in this thy day?" Or shall we try to realize our true mission, and come to the consciousness of God's kind intentions before it is too late? There is danger indeed of unduly modifying the interests and probable results of our own period, and of exaggerating every present crisis, and of glorifying our own particular mission. Many such a presumed crisis has passed, and the world abideth still. Heaven and earth have been invoked, in regard to the perils or prospects, now forgotten, or remembered by the thoughtful student or antiquary with the smile of pity or contempt. But surely "the end cometh."

There is a great temptation, also, to exaggeration among Americans. But aside from all these self-exalting exaggerations, in the sober and solemn light of facts and statistics, and the deep responsibilities they involve, we can hardly adequately measure the present, and especially the prospective greatness and consequent influence of our country. This impression is deepened by every view we can take of our country.

Look at the extent of territory, embraced in our present limits, immensely enlarged by recent annexations and acquisitions, requiring new editions of geography and alterations of maps every year to keep pace with our progress. Stretching already from the Atlantic to the Pacific, from wintry Maine to golden California! What a country! What an immense sea coast! And then a northern boundary of glorious inland seas—God's highways of commerce and communication from one extremity to the other!

The same impression is made, if we look at the *physical resources of our country*—the almost immeasurable capacity of sustaining population, and the almost infinitely varied productions of her soil. The natural resources of the American continent, it is computed, would afford sustenance to 3,600,000,000 inhabitants—four times the estimated present population of the globe. The Western country alone, could supply the whole world with bread-stuffs! I remember to have seen at one time, years ago, on the levee at St. Louis, a pile of such, half a mile long, and nine feet high!

Again, this impression is deepened, if we think of the *prospective population of our country.* It is conjectured, that fifty years from this time, we shall have a population of 75,000,000; and 100 years hence, of 275,000,000. In other words, where there is now one person, 50 years hence there will be 5, and 100 years from this time 16. And these will not be serfs or paupers, but American freemen, enlightened by education, conscious of their rights, and privileges, and powers, whether moulded and restrained by religion or not. Long before this latter period, our people, reinforced from the effete nations of the old world, will have filled up the vast basin of the Mississippi, and stretched across the Rocky Mountains to the shores of the Pacific, and be occupying centres of commercial wealth and of moral power, in close proximity to China and the East; and thus, empire and civilization, completing the mystic cycle, will reach the point whence they began their march westward round the world! Recent developments prove how speedily their centres can be moved half across a continent. Long before that time, too, the appliances of locomotion and transportation, now going forward, will be completed. Intelligence will be transmitted, with lightning speed, from one end of the continent to the other. From Boston and New-York, to San Francisco and Oregon City, dispatches can be sent in a few seconds, to hasten vessels of steam across to China, or Japan; and men may travel continuously from Maine to California without breaking the Sabbath.

Again, the same view is confirmed if we think of the *enterprise of our country.* How many hundreds of thousands of square miles of territory have we settled already; and how many tens of thousands of miles of canals and railroads have we constructed, and are now constructing and projecting! What immense primeval forests have given place, as by enchantment, to villages and towns and cities! See how agriculture, and commerce, and manufactures, and schools, and churches spring up along the path of American enterprise! In virtue of this characteristic the United States have already become the third, if not the second in the rank of commercial nations. The rapidity of our growth in this respect, throws Tyre, and Venice, and Holland, and England altogether into the shade. We now compete successfully with England in furnishing ships, engines and machinery for other nations. We excel and undersell her, in almost every market of the world; and by superior diplomacy, share with her in the results of her conquests in India and China. At the wharves of Pittsburg we fit out vessels for the trade of the Orinoco. American artisans build railroads for the Autocrat of Russia. They construct steamers for the Sultan of Turkey, and build and drive coaches across the desert for the Pacha of Egypt. We shall soon have lines of communication across the Isthmus of Darien, and a continuous communication to the Pacific, across the continent. But a few years ago, we carried on a war with one nation of the New World, and without inconvenience, fed at the same time the starving nations of the Old. Go where you will over the globe, and you will find Americans—amidst the icebergs of the Northern and Southern Poles, in the ports of China, India and Japan, in the Bosphorus and the Baltic, at the foot of the Himalayas and the Caucasus, at the World's Fair in London, and in search of Sir John Franklin!

In the same connection we may notice the element of power involved in *our unity*. With this immense population, and almost measureless resources, we shall have, unless evil counsels and sectional animosities prevail—which God in his mercy forbid—the influence of a united people. There is nothing like this in Europe. The ten toes of the great image, part iron and part clay, have no common principle of cohesion. European influence is frittered, from the fact that it has had no unity since the age of Charlemagne. Europe is but a congregation of nations of different languages, habits, and religions; and the traveller feels it as he passes from Britain to France, Spain, Germany, and Italy. But power, as it passes into our hands, comes to one people, speaking the same language, the language of Milton, Shakspeare, and the English Bible, having one literature, and one great common soul. Amidst all other ominous aspects, it is cheering to see how soon the process of homogeneity and nationalization is perfected here. Contrary to all antecedent reasoning, and in face of the Latin adage, "*Cœlum, non animum mutant qui trans mare currunt,*" it is a fixed fact, that men of all nations and languages, are here unified and Americanized! It seems as if the great God meant of all these materials to "make one new man," a type of humanity embracing the separate excellencies of all other forms. The element of power, for good or evil, involved in this unity and nationality, is immense. Already the name of America, embodying our institutions and the weight of our example, to the hope of millions, is strangely magical, in the ears and hearts of the savage and civilized portions of the Old World. What will it be, if fifty years hence finds us as now, "E Pluribus Unum;" when the new man, now comparatively in childhood, shall have grown to the measure of the stature of his destined proportions? What will be the influence of such a united and immense people, for good or evil, to scatter christianity and its temporal accompaniments and eternal consequences, or circulate pestilence and death over our world? In this view especially, the problem of perpetuated union, to the christian philanthropist, presents reflections of unparalleled intensity and interest. It is especially in the light of the the great idea, our country for the sake of the world, that the question of division and secession should be contemplated; and that Christians are concerned to know whether the centrifugal forces must necessarily be predominant, or whether one national life cannot be made to pervade this great land, notwithstanding differences of sentiment, and interests, and peculiar institutions.

If we look at these elements separately, especially if we combine them together on the most obvious principles, it must be allowed that our influence will be great; the weight of our example must be felt, the spirit of our institutions will be copied, and the type of our christianity or infidelity will be reproduced over the globe. We are set for the rise or the fall of many in our world. Nations unborn will rise up and call us blessed, if we become their benefactors, or load us with their heaviest curses, if we disappoint their rightful expectations. Oh! my country, after traversing thy beautiful prairies, and vast rivers, and inland seas, and viewing thy growing territory, and population, and future prospects, especially these elements of power; who that has a heart to love God, or his race, can refrain from praying, "God be merciful unto us, and bless us, and cause his face to shine upon us, that thy way may be known upon earth, thy saving health among all nations!"

We do believe—who can indeed help believing?—that if these elements of power are christianized and consecrated to the glory of God, and the spiritual good of men; if in our voyages and circumnavigations to every port where we traffic, and to every people where we transport our fabrics, we take the Bible, and a beautiful exemplification of its precepts in our own lives and principles; if American enterprise becomes synonymous with christian activity, and the love of Christ—the noblest and sweetest passion—comes to constrain commercial men, with a power and constancy equal to the love of money, which is the meanest; the way of God will soon be known on earth, and his saving health among all nations. On the other hand, if these elements be left to flow forth in selfish and vainglorious channels, unregulated by conscience and a sense of accountability; if the American name becomes identified in the apprehensions of the nations of the earth, with cunning, covetousness, and accumulation; then, no tongue can tell or heart conceive the influence for evil which will be exerted all over the earth, by our country.

We try to abound in hope; but we cannot altogether repress our fears, when we study the history of the spirit of trade in past ages, and trace, with facts before us, the premonitory symptoms of the decline and fall of the ancient centres of commercial greatness, which have successively figured and faded on the tableau of time. It is sad to muse on the elements of the glory of ancient Tyre; it is a solemn study, in view of the portraiture of the prophet Ezekiel, and the accomplished fact, to remember the late prediction of the Secretary of the Treasury in regard to this city, that "*soon the balance sheet of nations will be adjusted in New-York.*" We are a great people, indeed, and our greatness is increased on every side, and is increasing every decade. While traversing the mighty West, a man finds himself saying, "This is a great country—great for good or evil, for Christ or Antichrist!" Which shall it be? Whose shall be these prairies and cities, and this stalwart yeomanry? What part will they take in the great battle of principle? Whose forces will they swell in the last conflict? There is one reply every Christian would love to make, but there is an alternative also, in which all this enginery will be for evil—part of "the sublime mechanics of depravity," more potent, because more polished instruments of perdition.

Yes! American Christians, in the nature of the case and from the analogies of the past, it is safe to conclude that we must be a great people, but not necessarily or universally a holy people. This, with the blessing of God, depends on the efforts and sacrifices of those who have pledged themselves, and covenanted with God, to make the world's salvation their paramount concern, and every thing else subservient thereunto; and who, understanding aright the relations of our country to the world, as we have tried to depict them, have resolved to do their part under this stirring idea, "at such a time as this." For, let no man delude himself with the dream, alike contrary to fact and philosophy, that without evangelical influences and institutions, any thing else, however excellent, will preserve us as a people from ruin. There is no absolute warrant of safety in the peerlessness of our position, the grandeur of our mission, or the awful results of our failure; no promise of God, to prevent the most terrible catastrophe which fancy can conceive, or past history enables us to realize, provided we do not use the means which God has put in our power. Unless Christians, by their efforts and self-sacrificing zeal, make christian institutions, and their collateral evangelical influences commensurate with our widening population; unless we send the educated christian missionary along with the emigrant, and plant churches and Sabbath schools where the hand of enterprise has felled the forest or dotted the prairies with farms and villages ; our country, the star of hope and guidance to bewildered nations, will itself wander, and we shall lose an opportunity of blessing mankind, such as God never gave to any people since the world was created. Nothing but the power of the Gospel, made effectual in the hearts of men, and influencing them in all their relations, can save a free country like ours from destruction—a country where no despot in church or state does or dares force outward conformity to religious requirements; where the people rule, and make their own laws ; where public opinion is well nigh omnipotent, and independence of all control, human and divine, is the most striking and characteristic natural tendency. Here, the alternatives are moral principle,—making every man a law unto himself, without which outward law is a cobweb—the wildest anarchy, or military despotism. The Gospel planted these colonies with "seed sifted from three kingdoms." Gospel institutions have made us what we are, and nothing but the Gospel can preserve us from destruction, or enable us to fulfil our high destiny towards the race. It is not enterprise, or physical improvements, or a glorious constitution and good laws, or free trade, or a tariff, or railroads and steamships, or philosophy, or science, or taste ; but the grace of God, that bringeth salvation, appearing to every man, and inwrought into the heart of every man, that can save us from the fate of former republics, and make us a blessing to all nations.

The issues involved in this question depend very much, too, in our apprehension, on the character assumed and influence exerted by the West—on the fact, in other words, whether we supply its wastes and build there in a few years "the foundation of many generations." Religious institutions do not rise spontaneously, or necessarily keep pace with the growth of population. The human heart naturally does not value or secure evangelical influences. Its uncounteracted tendencies, if not to barbarism, are certainly to irreligion. Men every where, and in all ages, love darkness rather than light; especially the men who go out from the influences of churches and pastors, to seek their fortunes and dig for golden ore, and build them towers whose top will reach unto heaven. And such is the character of much of the population crowding the West. Scorched by the revivals, and restive under the restraints of other States, they go like Cain of old to found or find a city of repose. The restless spirit of change, the feeling of Daniel Boone, drives men from New England or New-York, to Illinois or Iowa, and then to Wisconsin and Minnesota, and then to Oregon and California. The outward wave is rolling onward, without regurgitation, till it meets the Pacific, where next to dash, God only knows! No one who has not travelled in the West can conceive aright of this subject, and the momentous issues involved in it. In the absorbing cares of business, the multiplicity of outward incitements and ever-recurring pageants, the uniform flow of affairs year after year, in older States and cities, we are prone to think that all is well, and the West will take care of itself. But to be able to pray the prayer of the text aright, every Christian ought, if possible, to see the West for himself. Good old deacons from New England, staid divines from churches where order and orthodoxy are triumphant, New-York merchants, retired civilians, and philanthropists, in order to realize their obligations, should go and survey the land where their children or children's children are to dwell—to be blessed or cursed, be blessings or curses, according as we do, or neglect to do our duty. This rapid transfer of population from the older settlements to the new, and the unparalleled tide of emigration from the Old World, to which recent events there will only give additional momentum, is a new development in the economy of nations, giving rise to new duties and responsibilities, and adjusting Christian obligation on a new scale of projection altogether.

> "No pent up Utica contracts our powers,
> But the whole boundless continent is ours,"

to care for, and to christianize. It is hard, after all we have read, to conceive with what rapidity the West is filling up with population. In some parts, "a nation is born in a day." Fifty years ago, a line drawn from Pittsburg north to Lake Erie, and southward along the Alleghany and Cumberland Mountains, to the Gulf of Mexico, would have embraced a white population of less than 500,000; now the State of Ohio alone contains a small fraction less than 2,000,000; Indiana little less than 1,000,000; Illinois 850,000. The total population of the States and Territories west of the Mississippi and north of the Ohio River, in 1830, was 1,840,000, less than Ohio alone at this time; while the entire population of Wisconsin amounting to upwards of 300,000, and of Iowa a little below 200,000, has been received since 1838. The city of St. Louis has regularly doubled its population every six years since 1831, when it numbered 6,000; at which time Chicago, Milwaukie and others, now young giants, had no existence. A brother in the Convention in Chicago, a few years ago, said, "In June you see one cabin on a prairie, passing along in September, you see forty."

It need not and ought not to be concealed, that in the West there is a singular "energy of error," and tendency to extremes of opinion on all subjects. Every thing there is on a large scale—rivers, forests, prairies. However philosophically accounted for, the same is true of their errors also. Errors, like weeds, grow rank in the human heart, without constant cultivation; while truth, like the valuable productions of the husbandman, requires constant, patient and diligent cultivation. The errors of the West are of gigantic proportions. Their leaders are bold, reckless and revolutionary. One of the most striking characteristics of the West, too, is the spirit of self-reliance, not to term it self-assurance, which manifests itself in church and state, among saints and sinners. They pronounce judgment on subjects which have perplexed the wisest heads of all time, with a self-satisfaction absolutely thrilling. They have, beyond all doubt, "the spirit of power," whether blended or not with the elements of "love and a sound mind." They are like their steamboats of high pressure, which have vast propelling power, whether they have prudent captains and sober crews or not. Like one of their representatives in Congress, many of them feel themselves head and shoulders above the rest of mankind. Every variety of human opinion, too, every heresy ever conceived in the human heart, or studied in the silent chamber in past ages, every plunge of radicalism, and every grade of infidelity is there. The errorist and revolutionist, from the older States and the other hemisphere, there find the material all plastic to their hand. The extremes of opinion, represented in our most sober communities, and trying in vain to work themselves into the religious and social structure, may there be carried out to the full extent, without regard to consequences. The mighty West seems like a great caldron, where every heterogeneous element is fermenting, foaming, and every now and then overflowing. Far off in these wilds you may meet travelling agencies for

New York books, a certain kind of literature, there known as the "Yellow Cover Literature," the miserable trash of paid scribblers—the staple productions of some large and flourishing eastern establishments. Whether we sleep over this subject, or wake up to a proper sense of duty and danger, while some ecclesiastics are fearing lest colportage will trench on their official prerogatives, there are bold and strong men there, "not afraid to speak evil of dignities," night and day sowing tares, scattering broadcast over the land their pestilent errors, loosening the bonds of morality, sapping the foundations of society, and baptizing the young with their baleful influences. What we do in this matter, we must do quickly, if at all—with our might, or the crisis is past. The preponderating political and religious influence of our country will soon be found, if it does not exist already, in the West. If we wait, if we trust these matters to chance, or please ourselves with dreamy anticipations, and do not rise and build, other hands will be found to give shape and character to this region, and seize these elements of power, and use them for their own purposes. There is a tide in human things, moments when the light dust may turn the balance of a nation's destiny one way or the other. And what but an educated, orthodox ministry, a ministry acquiring influence by intellectual superiority, and retaining it by intelligent piety and persevering efforts—just such a ministry as the Home Missionary Society proposes to send out—will meet the exigency created by these circumstances? What other conservative principles, than evangelical piety and institutions, can we trust amidst the tempests of passion and error which threaten to ingulf all that is dear to us as patriots and Christians, and all that is embosomed for our world, in the purity and perpetuity of American Christianity?

In addition to all we have said, you are aware that systematic overtures are making to bring our country, through the predominating power of the West, and thus our world, under Roman Catholic influence; to fight in that arena the battle of Popish or Protestant supremacy! On this point we are not, and never have been alarmists. We do not blame the Roman Catholics for their zeal. We honor them, on the contrary, for their consistency. They believe there is no salvation out of the church—meaning the Romish church; that the best temporal and civil interests of man are identified with the possession and prevalence of the true religion; and that every interest must be subordinated to the establishment and extension of Christ's kingdom on earth. With these principles, what else could we expect than the most vigorous and well-directed exertions to gain preponderance of power in our country, whose institutions are destined ultimately to spread over the world? They are fully cognizant of the facts and principles we have been stating. They know that our country must have immense influence, one way or the other, on the nations of the earth, and that the West is the destined seat of power. They lay their plans, and plant their institutions accordingly. They project their cathedrals, schools and colleges, on a scale of magnificence commensurate with our loftiest anticipations of the future. They build for future ages. They believe in perpetuity. They take hold of human nature by every handle to turn it to their purposes, and despise no avenues to human affection, or instrumentalities of human confidence. It is by no means uncommon to meet large Catholic churches where there are, now, scarcely any Catholic hearers; and female seminaries where there are scarcely any other than Protestant patrons. Verily, the prize is worth contending for—the privilege of a preponderating influence over this land, and thus over the world. As was said in the ancient games—"*Detur dignissimo*" —the prize to him that wins it. In this matter, God will not reverse the great principle of his economy, "The hand of the diligent maketh rich." It will not do for us to be forever quarreling with the Catholics, calling them bad names, accusing them of ambition, conspiracies, and what not, while we are doing nothing to establish Protestant institutions. It is pitiable to be groaning perpetually over Catholic progress and encroachments, while we lavish our wealth in schemes of self-glorification, without equaling, or at least emulating the zeal and benevolence of those whom we dread. We must rear better schools, give a better education to youth of both sexes, found libraries, sustain a learned and orthodox ministry so liberally, that they can cope successfully with the Jesuit. We must scatter evangelical books and a christian literature, over the whole field. Yea, we must personally labor in our respective posts, learn the luxury of making money to give away in large-hearted schemes of benevolence, if we would not see another generation, seduced by the gorgeous ceremonies and splendid pageants of Popery, forsaking the religion of their forefathers, and surrendering the institutions of America to the power of Antichrist.

Roman Catholics are in earnest. They say, "We must make haste; the moments are precious. America will one day be the centre of civilization, and shall truth or error establish there its empire? If Protestants are beforehand with us, it will be difficult to destroy their influence." Such is their avowed policy, and its expected results. Are we prepared to contemplate such a policy, and such results, with composure? Is it nothing to us whether truth, in their sense of the term, that is, Popery, or error, by which they mean the Protestant faith, Protestant morals, and Protestant institutions, shall be established in our land, and thus reign over the earth?

Catholics are united too, as well as earnest. Would to God, Protestants were also. We want a blessed evangelical alliance, with the spirit of the text for its motto, *Our country for the sake and salvation of our world.* Whatever denominational distinctions and lines of operation our imperfect sanctification and absorption in non-essentials may render still necessary or unavoidable, this great idea should outmaster and control every other, and make every one who loves Christ and labors for the salvation of our country, our brother beloved and honored, whether he casts out devils by our formularies, and follows with us or not.

A village in the West, for one half its population, which is Catholic, has one church and pastor, one Lord, one faith, one baptism ; the other half, which is Protestant, has five or six pastors and churches, and each has his separate "Psalm, doctrine, tongue, revelation and interpretation!" Yet, "God is not the author of confusion," but of peace, in all the churches of the saints.

Brethren, the mission of our country, and the alternative it involves, has not been conjured up for the occasion, but it is placed upon us by Providence, and grows necessarily out of the facts, principles and statistics we have been contemplating. In the light of the idea we have endeavored to elucidate and incorporate with your heart's deepest feelings, we can best see the reason and meaning of all God's past dealings with our country. In this aspect, our country must ever appear, to all capable of apprehending her position and relations, most lovely and glorious—as the signet in the right hand of God Almighty, by which he purposes to seal upon our fallen humanity its last type of beauty and blessedness. In the light of this purpose, we read with peculiar interest the facts of our antecedent history, civil and religious, from the beginning, hitherto. We can see why he planted these colonies; why he has preserved them; why he has interposed in answer to prayer in our darkest perils; why he has kept alive the spirit of piety, and granted us so many seasons of revivals; why he suggested the idea of voluntary associations; why he originated the Tract Society, and the glorious appendage of colportage; why, when the career of emigration first began, he put into the hearts of good men to form the Plan of Union; why, in advance of that unexampled career of expansion in recent times, which finds limits only by stretching from ocean to ocean, he originated this glorious Association of Home Missions, with its collateral blessings, to keep pace, if possible, with the march of an almost incalculable multiplication. Yes! it does seem as if God, our Heavenly Father, had prepared us, has been teaching us, for something great, and good, and glorious,—as Joseph was trained in youth, and then raised out of prison, to save much people alive in time of famine; and as David was called from tending sheep to lead the armies of the living God; and Hadassah was advanced from orphanage to the side of royalty to save her people, at an awful crisis.

Oh! my country! "Who knoweth whether thou"—lone orphan, cast out from thy fatherland and cut off from a mother's kindness in thy youth, and now Queen regnant, imperial and peerless—"hast not come to the kingdom for such a time," and for such a purpose "as this?" And after all, wilt thou fail to understand thy mission, and fall in with God's obvious purpose, and appreciate aright thy privilege and responsibility? In schemes of self-glorification or aggrandizement, wilt thou lose the glorious opportunity of impressing thine image, as God's signet, on the rest of the earth? O, holy brethren, partakers of the heavenly calling, American Christians of this generation! "Shall our country be the home of piety and virtue, or the mighty reservoir of irreligion and vice? Shall the voice of prayer and praise, or of cursing and blasphemy be heard throughout her borders? Shall our literature and science, and commerce and agriculture pay their tribute to the King of kings, or serve to foster to giant growth the worst passions of the human heart? Shall this great nation be rent with sectional jealousies and scarred with the judgments of the Most High, or shall its future millions, as they rise in successive generations, walk in the light of his countenance, and, appreciating themselves the value of civil and religious liberty, extend their blessings to every land illumed by the sun or laved by the sea?"

GOD BE MERCIFUL UNTO US, AND BLESS US, AND CAUSE HIS FACE TO SHINE UPON US; THAT THY WAY MAY BE KNOWN UPON EARTH, THY SAVING HEALTH AMONG ALL NATIONS.

AMERICAN HOME MISSIONARY SOCIETY.

The object of this Society is to assist congregations that are unable to support the Gospel ministry, and to send the Gospel to the destitute. It seeks and sends forth missionaries; by counsel and pecuniary aid, it encourages the people to help themselves; strengthens feeble churches, gathers new ones, settles pastors; and thus renders *permanent* the institutions of the Gospel.

The Society was organized in 1826, by delegates from the Presbyterian, Congregational, Associate Reformed, and Reformed Dutch denominations, and had then in its service 169 missionaries. The fifth year, the number of missionaries was 463—the eighth, 676—the sixteenth, 791—the twenty-fourth, 1,032. The first year's expenditure was $13,984—the fifth, $47,247—the eighth, $80,015—the sixteenth, $94,300—the twenty-fourth, $153,817 90.

The *twenty-fifth* year of its operations is briefly noticed in the following abstract from the last Annual Report, presented May 7th, 1851:

SUMMARY OF RESULTS.

More than one-third of those who were present at the organization of the Society a quarter of a century since, have ceased from their labors. Death has also removed, the last year, Rev. Calvin Chapin, D. D., and Rev. David Porter, D. D., Vice-Presidents of the Society; Rev. Henry White, D. D., one of its Directors; Knowles Taylor, Esq., its former Treasurer; and Rev. Washington Thacher, the Agent of the Society in Central New-York.

The Society has had in its service the last year, 1,065 ministers of the Gospel, in 26 different States and Territories: in the New England States, 311; the Middle States, 224; the Southern States, 15; the Western States and Territories, 515.

Of these, 640 have been the *pastors* or *stated supplies* of single congregations; and 425 have occupied larger fields. *Four* have ministered to congregations of *colored people;* and 41 have preached in foreign languages—10 to *Welsh,* and 29 to *German* congregations; and *two* to congregations of *Norwegians* and *Swedes.*

The *number of congregations* supplied, in whole or in part, is 1,820; and the aggregate of *ministerial service* performed is equal to 853 years.

The pupils in Sabbath schools and Bible classes amount to 70,000.

There have been *added to the Churches* 6,678, viz.: 3,855 by profession; and 2,823 by letter. Many of the Western Churches have been visited with the special effusions of the Spirit. *Seventy-seven* missionaries make mention in their reports of revivals of religion in their congregations; and 366 report 3,096 hopeful conversions.

THE TREASURY.

Resources.—The balance in the Treasury, April 1st, 1850, was $15,553 69. The *receipts* of the succeeding twelve months have been $150,940 25; making the resources of the year, $166,493 94.

Liabilities.—There was due to missionaries, at the date of the last report, $11,935 77. There has since become due, $151,515 41; making the total of liabilities $163,451 18.

Payments.—Of this sum, $153,817 90 have been *paid.* The remainder—$9,633 28—is still due to missionaries for labor performed. Towards liquidating these claims and redeeming the additional pledges on commissions which have not yet expired—making in all, $64,906 49—there is a balance in the Treasury of $12,676 04—the greater part of which was received near the close of the year, and is available only as a means of cancelling the present indebtedness of the Society to its missionaries.

PROGRESS.

Thirty-three more missionaries have been in commission than in any preceding year, and this increase has been mainly in the Western States and Territories; *forty-one more years of ministerial labor* have been performed; and *two hundred and forty-five* more congregations blessed with the preaching of the Gospel.

Forty-three churches have passed from a condition of dependence to that of *self-support; sixty houses of worship* have been completed; *fifty-five* others repaired; and the building of *forty* others commenced.

During the twenty-five years of the Society's labors, not far from 800 *churches,* which had been reared and nurtured by its instrumentality, have passed from the list of beneficiaries, and are now supporting their own Gospel institutions; some of which are among the strongest and most influential churches in the land.

AUXILIARIES AND AGENCIES.

The Report gives detailed statements of the prompt and liberal manner in which the views of the Executive Committee have been seconded by the local Boards of Agency, and by the State and other Auxiliaries,

While nearly all evince their activity by an increased number of Missionaries and of Churches assisted, they all report a larger number than in any previous year as having become independent of foreign aid. The sound and healthful growth of the missions is seen in the number and value of the houses of worship erected, in the increasing energy of measures to promote temperance, in the establishment of Sunday and Week-day schools, and in general, in the yearly progress of whatever promotes the stability of the churches and the order of society.

GENERAL VIEW.

The favor which God has shown to the Society during the past year, in preserving the lives of its officers and missionaries, and crowning their labors with such a measure of success, furnishes fresh occasion of gratitude, and new ground of encouragement. This record of the labors of the year, completes the history of this Society for a *quarter of a century.* Within this period, how has the field of its operations extended, and its work increased. Our frontier has receded from the banks of the Ohio to the shores of the Pacific. Seven States have been added to our confederacy, and 12,000,000 to our population. In all the elements of national importance, we have made unparalleled progress; and the work appropriate to this Society has increased in like proportion. And, though it has not accomplished all that with greater resources it might have accomplished, yet the wide fields where it has gathered rich harvests for Christ—the multitude to whom it has distributed the bread of life—the 3,000 churches it has aided, and the 100,000 souls it has gathered into the fold of the Great Shepherd, testify that it has not labored in vain.

In the prospective growth of our country for another quarter of a century, we foresee the accumulating responsibilities of this Society.—While, in the older States, it must "be watchful and strengthen the things that remain that are ready to die," it must also go forth "bearing precious seed," with the advancing tide of emigration, as it rolls toward the setting sun. In planting Gospel institutions in our great central valley, and on the shores of the Pacific, a work is to be done for Christ, such as he has intrusted to no other people. *It must not be delayed.* To this work let the friends of the Redeemer gird themselves anew.—Encouraged by his past favor and the promise of his presence and aid, let them prosecute this enterprise with increasing zeal and on a more extended scale.

www.ingramcontent.com/pod-product-compliance
Lightning Source LLC
LaVergne TN
LVHW011135110826
845150LV00008B/2365
* 9 7 8 1 4 1 8 1 9 4 5 2 9 *